This book belongs to

_____

Copyright © 2025 Grow Grit Press LLC. All rights reserved. No part of this book may be reproduced in any form without permission in writing from the publisher. Please send bulk order requests to info@ninjalifehacks.tv

Paperback ISBN: 979-8-89614-088-7
Hardcover ISBN: 979-8-89614-090-0
eBook ISBN: 979-8-89614-089-4

Printed and bound in the USA.
NinjaLifeHacks.tv

Anxious Alpaca worried a lot.
Her mind would spin, her thoughts would knot.
What if things went wrong today?
What if bad luck came her way?

At school, the teacher passed out tests.
Alpaca tried to do her best.
Her stomach churned, her hooves felt tight.
Her thoughts screamed,

"Oh no! What if I forget it all?
What if my brain just hits a wall?"
She bit her lip, she tapped her seat.
Her heart raced fast— *ba-bump, ba-beat.*)))

Calm Cow saw her friend's dismay,
and gently nudged her, "It's okay."
"I know three tricks to help you through.
A little trick called the *Three R's* will do!"

"First, *Recognize* what's in your mind.
Are worries helpful? Are they kind?
If thoughts feel big, just pause and say,
'I can't control it anyway.'"

Alpaca stopped and blinked a bit.
She thought, *Could that be true? That's it?*
Some worries weren't quite hers to steer.
Now, it all seemed very clear.

"Next," said Cow, "*Relax* instead.
Take deep breaths to soothe your head."
"In through your nose, out nice and slow,
breathe in calm, then let it go."

Alpaca tried—one breath, then two.
Her heartbeat slowed, her shoulders too.
The air felt cool, her mind felt light.
Hey... maybe Cow was kinda right.

"Last," said Cow, "*Refocus* your brain.
Think strong, kind thoughts to ease the strain.
Try, 'I'll do my best, and that's okay.'
Good thoughts can help fears go away."

Alpaca sat up tall and straight.
She whispered, *I can do this—great!*
She grabbed her pencil, took her time,
and *tried her best*—that felt just fine.

No tummy twists, no shaky knees,
no panicked thoughts, just gentle ease.
The *Three R's* worked—imagine that!
She smiled and thought as she sat.

That night, she lay tucked in her bed,
But worries swirled inside her head.
Then she recalled her brand-new way:

Recognize.

Relax.

Refocus today.

Now anytime her thoughts ran wild,
She'd use the *Three R's* and feel more mild.
Next time you feel your mind won't rest,
Try what Alpaca found works best!

Alpaca's Calm-Down Interactive Activities

Recognize Your Thoughts

What kinds of thoughts have you had today:

- What if I mess up?
- Everyone's looking at me.
- I'm not ready.
- I'll try my best!
- I've done hard things before.

Relax Your Body

Let's breathe like Calm Cow.

- Breathe in through your nose for 4 seconds
- Hold for 3 seconds
- Breathe out slowly for 6 seconds

Repeat 3 times. Trace a star with your fingertips every time you finish one:

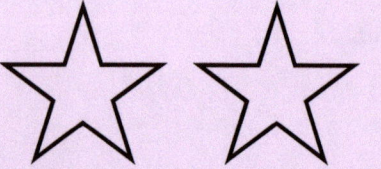

How does your body feel now?

Refocus with Kind Thoughts

Say one kind thing you'll say to yourself next time you feel anxious:

"I'll try my best, and that's _____."

Check out the Anxious Alpaca Lesson Plans at www.ninjalifehacks.tv

 @marynhin   @officialninjalifehacks
#NinjaLifeHacks

 Ninja Life Hacks

 Mary Nhin   Ninja Life Hacks

 @officialninjalifehacks

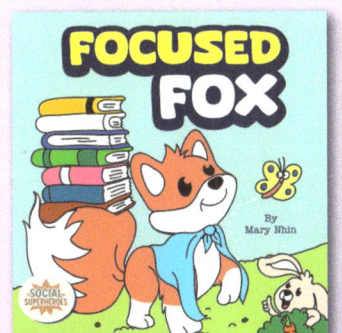

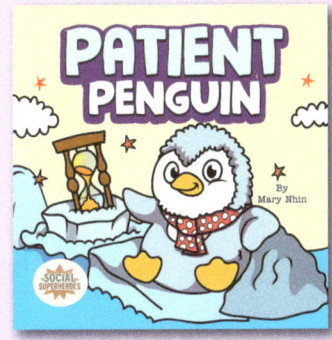
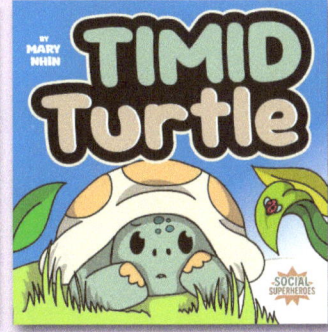

www.ingramcontent.com/pod-product-compliance
Lightning Source LLC
LaVergne TN
LVHW070434070526
838199LV00015B/511